AMY CONEY **BARRETT**

Supreme Court Justice

BY KATE CONLEY

CONTENT CONSULTANT
SCOTT S. BODDERY, JD, PhD
ASSISTANT PROFESSOR OF
POLITICAL SCIENCE AND PUBLIC LAW
GETTYSBURG COLLEGE

Essential Library

An Imprint of Abdo Publishing | abdobooks.com

abdobooks.com

Published by Abdo Publishing, a division of ABDO, PO Box 398166, Minneapolis, Minnesota 55439. Copyright © 2022 by Abdo Consulting Group, Inc. International copyrights reserved in all countries. No part of this book may be reproduced in any form without written permission from the publisher. Essential Library™ is a trademark and logo of Abdo Publishing.

Printed in the United States of America, North Mankato, Minnesota.
052021
092021

Cover Photo: Jim Lo Scalzo/AP Images
Interior Photos: Carolyn Kaster/AP Images, 4; Patrick Semansky/AP Images, 6, 58; Rob Crandall/Shutterstock Images, 11; Christopher Penler/Shutterstock Images, 13; Tom Williams/CQ Roll Call/AP Images, 14; Kevin Ruck/Shutterstock Images, 16; Shutterstock Images, 21; Susan Walsh/AP Images, 24, 81; Scott Boehm/AP Images, 26; Robert Franklin/South Bend Tribune/AP Images, 29; Erin Scott/Reuters/AP Images, 34; Ron Sachs/CNP/Newscom, 37; Ken Cedeno/CNP/AdMedia/Newscom, 38; Library of Congress, 40; Roger L. Wollenberg/Sipa USA/Newscom, 42; Ken Cedeno/CNP/Polaris/Newscom, 46; Bill Greenblatt/Hulton Archive/Getty Images, 48; Roman Babakin/Shutterstock Images, 50; Aaron Yoder/Shutterstock Images, 52; Kevin Dietsch/Pool/AP Images, 54, 91; Carlos Barria/Reuters/Newscom, 61; Jacquelyn Martin/Sipa USA/AP Images, 62; Pablo Martinez Monsivais/AP Images, 64; Fred Schilling/Supreme Court/AP Images, 69; Octavio Jones/Tampa Bay Times/AP Images, 71; Chip Somodevilla/Getty Images News/Getty Images, 72; Nicole Glass Photography/Shutterstock Images, 74; Cliff Owen/AP Images, 78; Graeme Jennings/Reuters/Alamy, 82; Alex Brandon/AP Images, 85; Stratos Brilakis/Shutterstock Images, 88; Yuri Gripas/Abaca/Sipa USA/AP Images, 93

Editor: Alyssa Krekelberg
Series Designer: Becky Daum

Library of Congress Control Number: 2020951572

Publisher's Cataloging-in-Publication Data

Names: Conley, Kate, author.
Title: Amy Coney Barrett: supreme court justice / by Kate Conley
Other title: supreme court justice
Description: Minneapolis, Minnesota : Abdo Publishing, 2022 | Series: Essential Lives | Includes online resources and index.
Identifiers: ISBN 9781532195938 (lib. bdg.) | ISBN 9781098216702 (ebook)
Subjects: LCSH: Barrett, Amy Coney--Juvenile literature. | Appellate courts--Juvenile literature. | Judges--Juvenile literature. | Women judges--Juvenile literature. | Women lawyers--Juvenile literature.
Classification: DDC 328.73092--dc23

CONTENTS

CHAPTER
ONE

A NEW JUSTICE

On October 26, 2020, the White House buzzed with activity. The White House staff, along with the rest of the nation, was waiting to hear from the US Senate. Exactly one month earlier, President Donald Trump had nominated Amy Coney Barrett to fill an empty seat on the US Supreme Court. A group of senators had spent days interviewing her in public hearings. Now, the entire Senate was ready to vote on whether to add her to the court. Shortly before eight o'clock that evening, the Senate approved Barrett. This made her the newest justice on the Supreme Court.

An hour later, hundreds of lawmakers and other guests gathered on the south lawn of the White House. The lit-up building glowed dramatically against the night sky, and dozens of flags hung from the portico. A military band began to play "Hail to the Chief," and moments later President Trump walked out of the White House to greet the crowd. Supreme Court justice

Amy Coney Barrett stands with President Donald Trump in front of the White House the night she's confirmed as a US Supreme Court justice.

Barrett became the fifth woman to serve on the US Supreme Court.

Clarence Thomas and newly confirmed Justice Barrett joined him.

Trump stepped up to the podium. He welcomed the guests and offered his thanks to those who had supported Barrett. He also restated his confidence in her abilities to serve as a justice. "Over the past few weeks, the entire world has seen Justice Barrett's deep knowledge, tremendous poise, and towering intellect. She answered questions for hours on end. Throughout her entire confirmation, her impeccable credentials were unquestioned, unchallenged, and obvious to all," said Trump. "Justice Barrett has made clear she will issue rulings based solely upon a faithful reading of the law and the Constitution as written, not legislate from the bench."[1]

When he finished speaking, Trump stepped back from the podium. Justices Barrett and Thomas stepped forward. Barrett's husband, Jesse, joined them with a Bible in his hand. He held it out to his wife, who placed her left hand upon it and raised her right hand. She faced Justice Thomas, who administered the constitutional oath of office. Barrett promised to do her job faithfully and defend the US Constitution.

The crowd applauded, and Barrett took her place at the podium. "The oath that I have solemnly taken tonight means, at its core, that I will do my job without any fear or favor, and that I will do so independently of both the political branches and of my own preferences," Barrett said. "I love the Constitution and the democratic republic that it establishes, and I will devote myself to preserving it."[2]

A Swift Ascent

Barrett's swearing-in ceremony was the high point of a career that had risen rapidly. In the span of four years, Barrett had gone from a law professor, to a federal judge, to a Supreme Court justice. She first drew national attention in 2017. That year, Trump appointed her as a federal judge on the US Court of Appeals for the Seventh Circuit. A court of appeals can review decisions made by district courts. As with all appointments to this court, the Senate Judiciary Committee held a public hearing on Barrett. The hearing grew heated over some points. Barrett's Catholic faith was at the center of many people's questions. Some wondered whether she would

THE CONFIRMATION PROCESS

A prospective Supreme Court justice goes through a specific legal process before he or she can join the court. On average, this process takes between two and three months. It starts with the president. The US Constitution says the president "shall nominate, and by and with the Advice and Consent of the Senate, shall appoint . . . Judges of the Supreme Court."[4]

Once the president nominates a candidate, the Senate typically begins its work. The Senate Judiciary Committee meets to learn more about the candidate's background. Then the committee holds a hearing. Members of the committee interview the nominee. They vote on the nomination. If the vote passes, the nomination goes to the Senate floor. If the Senate approves the nomination, the candidate is then sworn in and begins working on the Supreme Court.

be able to separate her faith from the law when deciding cases. They worried her religious beliefs would influence her rulings on contentious topics, such as those involving abortions. The Senate ultimately confirmed her, and Barrett took her place as a federal judge.

Barrett's name next appeared in national news in 2018 when Supreme Court justice Anthony Kennedy retired. Trump needed to pick a replacement, and Barrett had made it on his short list of potential nominees. In the end, Trump decided to nominate Brett Kavanaugh to replace Kennedy. The Senate later confirmed Kavanaugh, and Barrett continued to work on the appeals court.

Although Trump had passed on Barrett for the time being, he still hoped to eventually get her on the Supreme Court. Some people wondered whether Trump would nominate her if Justice Ruth Bader Ginsburg, who was 85 years old in 2018, left the court. The Constitution doesn't limit how long a Supreme Court justice can serve, so people have no way of knowing when a vacancy may open up. Historically, Supreme Court vacancies only occur when a justice steps down or passes away. Trump hoped he would have the opportunity to fill another court spot during his presidency. If given the chance, Trump wanted to nominate Barrett.

Confirmation

Ginsburg had served on the court since 1993. During this time, she had become something of a hero to many Americans on the left side of the political spectrum. She had earned a reputation for her liberal and outspoken opinions. Ginsburg championed women's equality, same-sex marriage, and civil rights for a variety of marginalized groups. However, her views made her a controversial figure to some. Many Republicans wanted her to be replaced with a more conservative justice when she left the court. They saw Barrett as someone who would fill that role.

Ginsburg had been treated for cancer in her colon, lungs, pancreas, and liver. Throughout her

Ruth Bader Ginsburg was 60 years old when
she joined the US Supreme Court.

health struggles, Ginsburg continued working on the
court. In July 2020, Ginsburg announced that she
was undergoing cancer treatment once again. On
September 18, 2020, Ginsburg passed away.

Trump was making a campaign stop in Minnesota
when he received word of Ginsburg's death. Upon

learning the news, Trump said, "She led an amazing life, what else can you say? She was an amazing woman— whether you agreed or not—she was an amazing woman who led an amazing life."[5] He later tweeted about Ginsburg, praising her sharp mind and her notable dissents. While the nation mourned one of its justices, the work of selecting her replacement fell to Trump. Filling Ginsburg's shoes wouldn't be an easy task.

Republicans wanted to appoint another conservative justice to the Supreme Court while they had control of the Senate. If a nomination is brought to the Senate for approval, senators vote on whether to appoint the nominee to the Supreme Court. Starting in 2017, only a simple majority of senators was needed to approve a nominee.

Every four years, approximately one-third of senators are up for reelection. At the time of Ginsburg's death, the 2020 election was looming closer, and it was possible that the Senate could come under the control of the Democrats. If that happened, even if Republican president Trump won a second term in the 2020 election, he likely wouldn't be able to get his Supreme Court pick past a Democratic Senate.

Some people protested the growing conservative leaning of the Supreme Court.

Trump had already appointed two conservative justices: Neil Gorsuch and Brett Kavanaugh. Adding Barrett would make the court more conservative than it had been since 1950. This had the potential to create far-reaching effects. It would make overturning controversial rulings a real possibility. For example, Trump and many other conservatives hoped to overturn cases such as *Roe v. Wade*, which ruled that it

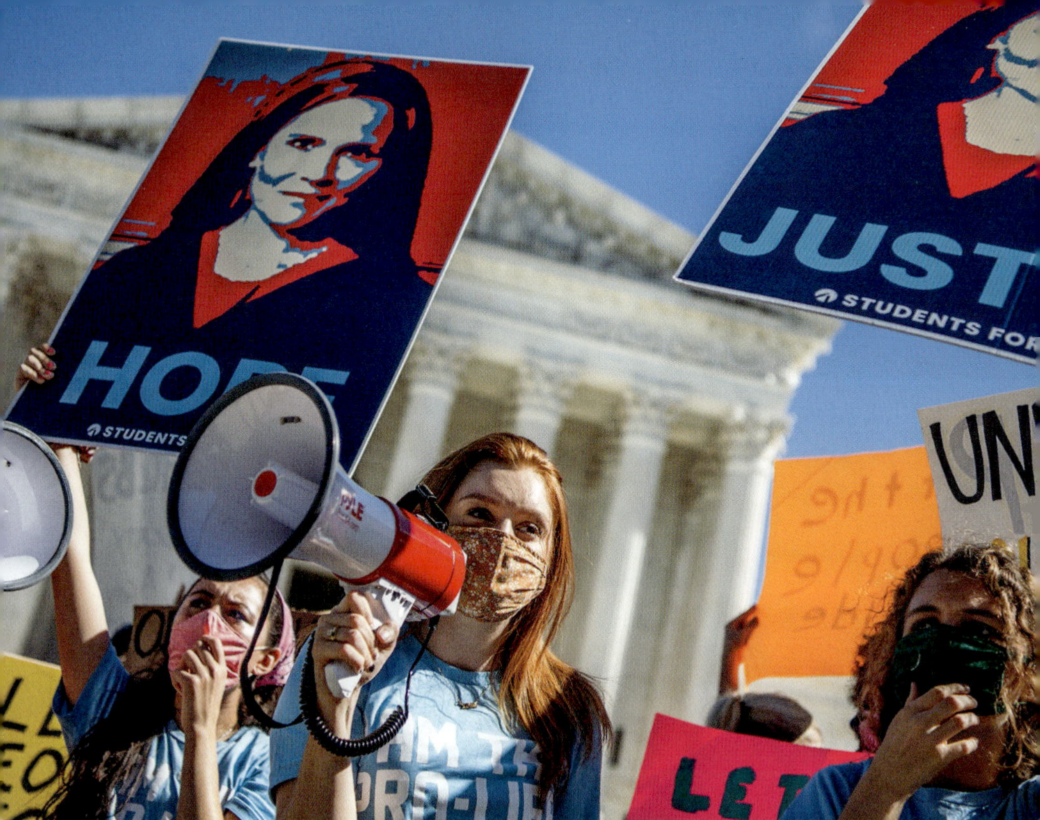

Many people saw Barrett's nomination to the Supreme Court as a sign of hope for pro-life groups.

was unconstitutional to unduly prohibit women from accessing abortions. Before Barrett's nomination, the Supreme Court was already leaning conservative. If Barrett was confirmed, the court would have even stronger ties to conservative ideologies, and this was a polarizing issue in the run-up to the 2020 election.

Once again, Trump put Barrett on his short list of potential nominees. Many of the conservatives that Trump represented liked what they saw in Barrett. She had an impressive legal background. She also spoke openly about her faith and was the mother of seven children. Conservatives began to tout her as a role model for the modern, professional woman, and Trump officially nominated her on September 26, 2020. Barrett went through the confirmation hearing process with the Senate Judiciary Committee. The overall Senate vote was largely along party lines, and Barrett was ultimately confirmed.

"I have no illusions that the road ahead of me will be easy, either for the short term or the long haul," said Barrett. "I never imagined that I would find myself in this position. But now that I am, I assure you that I will meet the challenge with both humility and courage."[6] She noted that the sources of her courage and humility were deeply rooted in her family and her faith.

A LIFELONG APPOINTMENT

Some people believe that nominating a Supreme Court justice is one of the president's most important duties. A justice can influence the court and its decisions for years to come. That's because Supreme Court justices hold their positions for life. They never have to face reelection or term limits. That gives them the freedom to make unpopular rulings in cases without fear of not being reelected. Justices can focus on what is just and legal under the law rather than what is the popular opinion. The goal of this system is to keep them focused on justice instead of being swept up in politics.

CHAPTER
TWO

GROWING UP

Amy Vivian Coney was born on January 28, 1972, to Michael and Linda Coney. She was the oldest of the family's seven children. The Coney family lived in Metairie, a suburb just outside of New Orleans, Louisiana. Before Amy was born, her mother worked as a high school French teacher and her father worked as a lawyer for Shell Oil Company. Their career choices greatly impacted Amy, and she said years later, "I thought the two coolest things to be would be a high school French teacher or English teacher or a lawyer."[1]

Michael and Linda were committed to their Catholic faith. Michael's religion had been especially important to him ever since his mother passed away during his teenage years. As an adult, his Catholic faith was one of the driving forces in his life. When Amy was ten years old, her father became a deacon. He and Linda also joined a faith community called People of Praise. This group became a central part of the Coney family's life.

New Orleans is the biggest city in Louisiana, and it's also an important port city.

People of Praise is an ecumenical group. That means all Christians can join, regardless of what kind of church they attend, although 90 percent of its members are Catholic.[2] The group calls itself a covenant community. Members make a covenant—or promise—to support the group for their whole lifetimes. They agree to serve, pray, and work together. Many members often choose to live near each other to make this easier. The Coney family home in Metairie was on the same block as those of several other families who were part of People of Praise.

This community became a vital part of the Coney family's life and affected aspects of the family's decisions, including the choices Amy's father made about his career. When Amy was around 13 years old, her father received a promotion at Shell Oil Company. It would require the family to move from

Louisiana to Houston, Texas. At the time, the Coneys had six young children. The job promotion would be great for Michael's career, but it would also disrupt his family's life. "This is awful," Michael said to Linda when telling her the news about his promotion. "A move to Houston means life for our family will never be the same."[3]

Michael ultimately accepted the position. Rather than move the whole family, he decided to commute between New Orleans and Houston, which is about a five hour drive one way. He quickly realized it would not work for his family. After three months in Houston, he quit the job. "Our life was in a covenant community in New Orleans," Michael said, reflecting on the promotion years later. "For the sake of our children

PEOPLE OF PRAISE

People of Praise started as part of the charismatic renewal, a movement that was spreading in some Christian churches in the late 1960s. People active in the charismatic renewal reported deep spiritual experiences, such as speaking in tongues or physical healings. In 1971, a group of people in South Bend, Indiana, formed People of Praise based on this movement. They worked to bring the charismatic renewal to the Catholic Church. According to People of Praise, the charismatic renewal has affected more than 30 percent of US Catholics.[4] In 2020, People of Praise had approximately 1,700 members worldwide.[5]

and ourselves, we needed committed relationships with
other Christians who were serious about their faith."[6]
Shell Oil Company later rehired Michael with the
promise that he could keep his promotion and stay in
New Orleans.

Going to School

Amy and her siblings attended St. Catherine of Siena
Catholic School when they were young. It was the school
affiliated with the local parish where her family attended
church. Then Amy attended St. Mary's Dominican High
School, which is an all-girls Catholic school. The women
in Amy's family had attended this school for generations.
Amy thrived during her high school years, later saying,
"I loved being at an all-girls school. It was really, I think,
freeing. I formed really close friendships. We could be
very competitive with one other academically. There
was just a lot of freedom."[7]

During her time there, Amy served as vice president
of the student body and wrote for the school newspaper.
The coursework was challenging. By her junior year,
she was taking a class on social justice. Part of the
coursework was reading papal encyclicals. These are
letters written by the pope—who is the head of the

There are thousands of Catholic schools in the United States.

Catholic Church—to all Catholics. The letters cover topics related to faith, morals, and world events. Amy read papal encyclicals on nuclear weapons, the rights of workers, and economic inequality. She also learned about the Church's beliefs on topics such as abortion and contraception.

The woman who taught the social justice course, Royann Avegno, influenced Amy in more than just academics. Avegno was the mother of eight children, and she often shared stories about them with her class. Seven of her eight children had been adopted, and they had various medical conditions and other special needs. Avegno brought one of her sons into class one day. He could not speak or stand. Avegno reminded her students about human dignity and his value as a

Popes have been writing letters to members of the Catholic Church for many years. The first official papal encyclical was written by Pope Benedict XIV in 1740. Since that time, popes have issued hundreds of encyclicals. The encyclicals do not create new core beliefs, but they do provide the Catholic Church's official stance on a variety of issues. They can touch on many different topics, including those related to global warming and nuclear war.

person. The encounter left a deep impression on Amy's views of adoption and children with special needs.

Rhodes College

Barrett graduated from high school in 1990. She knew she wanted to go to college, but she wasn't sure where. Her parents were paying private school tuition for her six younger siblings, so she wanted to pick a college that she and her family could afford. In addition, because she had a close-knit family, she didn't want to go to school too far from New Orleans. Barrett decided on a small liberal arts school called Rhodes College in Memphis, Tennessee, which had offered her a scholarship. It was a six-hour drive between the campus and her family's home.

While at Rhodes, Barrett majored in English and minored in French. It was an easy decision for her.

"Ever since I was a little girl, I've loved to read and write and being an English major allowed me to do that," Barrett said when reflecting on her time at Rhodes.[8] In addition to studying, Barrett was involved in many other activities. She joined the Kappa Delta sorority, participated in Model United Nations, served on the student honor council, and belonged to the Catholic student group. Barrett also worked on campus. She was a resident adviser in the dorms and a tour guide for prospective students.

As she neared graduation, Barrett had to decide what her next step in life would be. The two options that seemed most promising to her were to become an English professor or a lawyer. During her senior year, she pondered her options. She made a list of pros and cons and went back and forth on what each career

Barrett was a distinguished student at Rhodes College, earning awards and a spot in the college's Hall of Fame.

would look like for her. Barrett ultimately decided to attend law school. "I liked that law would enable me to do the reading and writing that I loved, but also be involved in real-world things—real-world policy and shaping of society in a more direct way than I thought teaching English literature would," she said.[10]

With that decided, Barrett began applying to law schools. Her professors encouraged her to choose elite schools on the east coast, such as Harvard University in Massachusetts. But she had her sights set on a different prestigious institution. When Barrett graduated from Rhodes College in 1994, she moved to South Bend, Indiana, where she enrolled at the University of Notre Dame's law school. It was there that her passion and skill for the law would quickly gain attention.

CHAPTER
THREE

NOTRE DAME LAW SCHOOL

Barrett began her studies at Notre Dame in 1994. It didn't take long for other students and professors to take notice of her intellect as well as her passion for the law. Douglas Kmiec was one of Barrett's professors during her first year of law school. He taught a number of courses, including some that were unpopular but required. These courses often dealt with historical parts of the law. Over the years, many of Kmiec's students bristled against learning this part of the law, but Barrett did not. Instead, she dug into it with enthusiasm.

Barrett's willingness to embrace challenging topics rather than complain about them drew Kmiec's attention. He described her as a student who took joy in gaining knowledge and in learning to see situations from different perspectives. She did not shy away from the demanding historical research required to gain an understanding of the law. Not only that but Barrett also

Around 12,000 students attend the University of Notre Dame each year.

had an ability to explain her opinions in a way that was remarkably persuasive.

Kmiec remembered one specific incident where Barrett's intellect caught his attention. He was teaching a class on property laws. It involved learning about statutes and provisions that go back centuries. One of those laws—the Law of Perpetuities—was especially complex. It involved a detailed formula that was often hard for students to grasp, but it wasn't difficult for Barrett.

Not only did Barrett understand the concept quickly, she discovered an error in the course materials. According to Kmiec, "She identified in the casebook where the author, a very distinguished author . . . had made a mistake and propounded an answer that Amy demonstrated conclusively could not be. One knew immediately in that early classroom two things: Amy loved the law, and

Barrett spoke at the 2018 commencement
ceremony of Notre Dame Law School.

she was not hesitant at all to take on the most difficult
problems, and often, because of her intellect, show the
way to a better answer."[1]

Other professors, such as John Garvey, quickly
noticed Barrett's aptitude for the law too. Garvey had
Barrett as a student in his class on the First Amendment.

At that time, Garvey did not know Barrett by name, but that would change quickly. "On the final exam, someone—the blue books were anonymous—had written an answer so impressive that I rushed to share it with one of my colleagues. This student, I said, gave a response to my own question much better than the one I had come up with myself. That student was Amy Coney."[2]

Studying at Notre Dame helped Barrett sharpen her intellect, and it also helped shape her outlook on life. In 2019, Barrett discussed how Notre Dame did this when she joined fellow graduates from Notre Dame Law School at an event titled "A Conversation with Judge Amy Coney Barrett." It was organized by the Notre Dame Club of Washington, DC. Megan Wold, the moderator of the event, sat across from Barrett. For 45 minutes, Wold asked Barrett a variety of questions. They covered everything from her childhood to her work on the US court of appeals. It was a chance for Barrett to talk about her life and work in her own words.

Of special interest to the people gathered there that night was Barrett's decision to attend law school at the University of Notre Dame. When Wold asked

Barrett what had brought her to Notre Dame, Barrett smiled. "I'm a Catholic. I always grew up loving Notre Dame. What Catholic doesn't?" she asked. "And when I decided to go to law school, I really wanted to choose a place where I felt like I was not going to be just educated as a lawyer, but I wanted to be in a place where I felt like I would be developed and inspired as a whole person. And I think, what better place than Notre Dame for that?"[3]

Becoming an Originalist

Throughout law school, Barrett was exposed to a variety of ways that lawyers and judges interpret the US Constitution. In her first year of law school, she took a course on constitutional criminal procedure. It is an area of the law that is concerned with how criminal cases are investigated, prosecuted, and judged. The class was

Barrett's first real exposure to constitutional cases. As she learned more, Barrett began to lean toward a certain way of interpreting the Constitution. She began to see herself as an originalist.

Originalists view the Constitution as a fixed document. According to Glenn C. Smith, a constitutional law professor at California Western School of Law, "The 'original intent' approach seeks to the extent possible to base [court] decisions on the

ORIGINALISTS AND MODERN LIFE

Originalists believe the Constitution does not change and must be interpreted the way it was originally intended. However, the Constitution was written before many of today's technologies existed. Some people question how it's possible to apply these old laws to new ways of life. Justice Neil Gorsuch, who is an originalist, explained how this works in a 2019 essay for *Time*:

> As originally understood, the First Amendment protected speech. That guarantee doesn't just apply to speech on street corners or in newspapers; it applies equally to speech on the Internet. Or consider the Fourth Amendment. As originally understood, it usually required the government to get a warrant to search a home. And that meaning applies equally whether the government seeks to conduct a search the old-fashioned way by rummaging through the place or in a more modern way by using a thermal imaging device to see inside. Whether it's the Constitution's . . . protection of speech, or its restrictions on searches, the meaning remains constant even as new applications arise.[4]

constitutional concepts of those who drafted the relevant language. Originalists believe that the Constitution's central purpose was to enshrine core rights and understandings."[5] In other words, originalists interpret the Constitution the way it was intended when written.

This viewpoint is in contrast to that of people who are living constitutionalists. They believe constitutional law should change with the times to mirror new values and circumstances found in society. A decision made by living constitutionalism can be seen in the 2015 court case *Obergefell v. Hodges*, which legalized gay marriage. John Bursch was the Michigan solicitor general between 2011 and 2013, and he argued many cases in front of the Supreme Court. He noted that living constitutionalists "would say that the same-sex marriage decision is the perfect example of why courts need some flexibility to depart from the text, structure, and original intent [of the Constitution]."[6]

The Fourteenth Amendment affirms people's equal protection under the law. When the amendment was ratified in 1868, lawmakers were likely not aiming to legalize same-sex marriage. However, a living constitutionalist believes constitutional law should evolve with societal and cultural changes, such as the

As an originalist, Barrett strives to interpret the Constitution
the way it was intended when ratified.

acceptance of same-sex marriage. Originalists and living
constitutionalists are neither right nor wrong; they just
have different ways of interpreting the Constitution.
The way a person views a situation through one of these
lenses can affect the outcome of a case.

As she learned more, Barrett's understanding of
the law continued to line up closely with originalists'.
"I wasn't familiar when I entered law school with

originalism as a theory," Barrett said when speaking
to students at Hillsdale College in 2019. "But I found
myself as I read more and more cases becoming more
and more convinced that the opinions that I read that
took the originalist approach were right."[7]

Graduation and the Future

Barrett graduated from law school in 1997. As in
the past, she had excelled academically. She earned
her law degree *summa cum laude*, which means "with
highest distinction." As the top student in her class,
she earned the Hoynes Prize, which is the highest
honor for a student at Notre Dame Law School. As
a student, Barrett had also been a Kiley Fellow. The
Kiley Fellowship is the law school's most prestigious
scholarship. Barrett had also served as executive editor
of *Notre Dame Law Review*, which is a student-run journal
that provides articles on legal matters.

All of these things would help Barrett find a good
job. Before graduating, Barrett also turned to Notre
Dame professors Patrick Schiltz and William Kelley
for advice on her next steps. At that time, conservative
leaders were working to develop a pool of talented
female and minority lawyers. Their goal was to bring

these new faces to the federal courts. It was an attempt to change the image the Republican Party had of only promoting white men.

In the past, both Schiltz and Kelley had worked as law clerks for federal judges. They drew upon their contacts to help connect Barrett with her first job in the legal field. As she left her student life at Notre Dame behind, Barrett headed to Washington, DC, to begin a clerkship with Judge Laurence H. Silberman.

Laurence H. Silberman, *right*, is a distinguished judge who
has held other government roles such as undersecretary
of labor and deputy attorney general.

CHAPTER
FOUR

LIFE AS A CLERK

Judge Laurence H. Silberman had been reluctant to hire Barrett as a clerk. It wasn't because of her academic performance, as she had an outstanding record at Notre Dame. At first, Silberman hesitated to hire her because she had not gone to a more elite school. He typically only hired clerks from Harvard, Yale University in Connecticut, and the University of Chicago. Silberman later recalled Patrick Schiltz and William Kelley telling him, "You're such a snob, your law clerks are largely from Harvard, and we have a woman at Notre Dame who's first in her class."[1] Kelley maintained that if Barrett had gone to Harvard, she would have finished at the top of her class there too. Silberman heard enough good things about Barrett that he hired her in 1997 without making her go through the interview process.

Silberman worked as a judge on the US Court of Appeals for the District of Columbia Circuit. He had served in that position since 1985, when President

Barrett worked hard during her time as a law clerk. This helped her later on in her career.

President Ronald Reagan nominated more than 300 judges during his time in office.

Ronald Reagan had appointed him. Barrett would be working as Silberman's clerk. Being a law clerk is similar to being an apprentice. A new member of the profession works with an experienced leader.

Barrett's clerkship with Silberman lasted for one year. She excelled at her job, and halfway through the clerkship, Silberman called Kelley. "You undersold her," he told Kelley, pretending to be angry.[2] In later interviews, Silberman went on to praise Barrett as someone who has "brilliant analytic skills combined with an innate sense of decency and kindness."[3] As Barrett's clerkship with Silberman drew to a close, he recommended her as a clerk to Supreme Court justice Antonin Scalia.

Clerking for Scalia

President Reagan had appointed Scalia to the Supreme Court in 1986. As a justice, Scalia became well known for his conservative, originalist legal viewpoints. He had a reputation for having a good sense of humor and a quick wit, but he was a strong, serious presence on the bench. Scalia had an aggressive style of asking questions during oral arguments. When writing opinions, he often used sharp, biting, and even sarcastic

DUTIES OF A LAW CLERK

Clerkships are a good start for new lawyers because they provide a wide range of real-world experiences. The main duties of law clerks are legal research and analysis. These duties are related to the cases the judge is preparing to hear or rule upon. Writing is another large part of the job for law clerks. Clerks draft memos, opinions, briefs, and instructions for juries. Editing is also an important duty. Clerks make sure that official writings from the judge are free of mistakes and correctly cite the law.

Antonin Scalia, *left*, served on the Supreme Court for 30 years.

comments. Though Scalia's style drew criticism, many people also greatly respected his work.

Scalia had been on the Supreme Court for more than a decade when Barrett began working for him in 1998. Clerking for Scalia was a dream job for Barrett. "I picked up the phone and the voice on the other end said, 'please hold for Justice Scalia,'" Barrett recalled about the moment she learned of the clerkship. "I was so excited; my heart was racing. He comes on the line and starts asking me how I am and what's new. Then he says he wanted me to clerk for him after I completed my clerking with Judge Silberman. I immediately said 'yes' and began thanking him over and over again."[4]

One of her first experiences as Scalia's clerk was in the cert pool. Each year the Supreme Court receives an average of 7,000 petitions for certiorari. These petitions, known as certs, are requests for the court to hear cases. In an average year, the Supreme Court only hears between 100 and 150 cases.[5] To help sort through which of the 7,000 cases will be heard, some justices use the cert pool as a procedural step to increase efficiency.

Supreme Court clerks read through the certs. They write a summary of the arguments for each side of a case. They give the writings to the justices, who then decide which cases to hear. "Justice Scalia participated in the cert pool, so you start in the summer and you're thrown into writing memos that you know will be circulated," recalled Barrett. "At the time, eight of the nine justices were in the cert pool. So it's a little

CLERKS WHO BECAME JUSTICES

Working as a clerk for a Supreme Court justice is viewed by many people to be a great honor. Over the court's history, nine justices had previously served as clerks for justices on the Supreme Court. They were Byron R. White, William H. Rehnquist, John Paul Stevens, Stephen G. Breyer, John G. Roberts, Elena Kagan, Neil Gorsuch, Brett Kavanaugh, and Amy Coney Barrett.

stressful when you realize you're writing things that eight Supreme Court justices are going to be reading."[6]

The cert pool was just one part of the job. Barrett, along with Scalia's three other clerks, would join Scalia in his chambers before he heard a case in court. He would ask the clerks for their opinions on the case. Scalia didn't want the clerks to automatically agree with him just because he was their boss. He wanted to hear their true ideas, even if they disagreed with him. "He wanted you to say what you thought," said Barrett. "And so disagreeing with him as I sometimes did and pushing back and going back and forth with someone like Justice Scalia really taught me a lot," she said.[7]

Scalia's way of interpreting the Constitution impacted

Barrett. In law school she had become an originalist, and Scalia was a vocal proponent of originalism as well. By working with him, she learned how he used this method of interpreting the Constitution in real cases. "His approach very much emphasized the primacy of text. His view was that . . . the Constitution means what it meant to those who ratified it. . . . If we change the law now to comport with our current understandings or what we want it to mean, then it ceases to be the law that has democratic legitimacy," Barrett said.[9] She added that Scalia believed changes to laws—whether through constitutional amendments or statutory changes—should come from the state and federal governments rather than the judiciary branch. Scalia's teachings left their mark on Barrett, who largely adopted his judicial philosophy.

Marriage and a New Job

Barrett's clerkship with Scalia ended in 1999, but it was just the beginning for her in another part of her life. That year, she married Jesse Barrett. Like his wife, Jesse was a lawyer. He was also a member of the same religious community Barrett had grown up in—People

of Praise. The two had met in the 1990s when they were
both law students at Notre Dame.

The newlyweds each took new jobs near
Washington, DC. Jesse took a clerkship with Judge
Paul Niemeyer. He worked on the US Court of Appeals
for the Fourth Circuit, which is based in Richmond,
Virginia. Barrett took a job at a private law firm called
Miller, Cassidy, Larroca & Lewin. Scott Nelson,
who was in charge of hiring there, said Barrett's
impressive background as a clerk for both Silberman
and Scalia made her an exciting candidate. "She was
the kind of person that I think most law firms would be
delighted to hire as a first-year associate at that time,"
Nelson recalled.[10]

At the law firm, Barrett worked on criminal,
commercial, and constitutional cases. She researched,
wrote briefs, and conducted depositions. Most of the
cases did not gain much national attention, but that
all changed in 2000 when Barrett started to work on
a high-profile case. Her law firm was representing
presidential candidate George W. Bush, who was
involved in a legal battle that centered on the presidential
election results. Barrett traveled to Florida, where

Jesse Barrett, *left*, holds the Bible that Amy Coney Barrett used during her Supreme Court swearing-in ceremony.

Al Gore, *left*, and George W. Bush, *right*, participated in presidential debates before the 2000 election.

thousands of ballots were being recounted to determine whether Bush or Al Gore won the US presidency.

In late 2020, Barrett had not spoken at length about her role in the case. She is believed to have helped with

research and briefings. The case, *Bush v. Gore,* went
to the Supreme Court, which ruled in favor of Bush.
This decision ultimately made him the forty-third
US president. Despite the excitement of a big case like
Bush v. Gore, Barrett did not stay in private practice
for long. Instead, she began to think about returning
to academia.

BUSH V. GORE

In 2000, Republican governor of Texas George W. Bush and Democratic vice president Al Gore ran for president. The election was close, and the presidency came down to who won Florida. There, Bush had won by only 0.01 percent of the votes.[11] This narrow margin triggered a recount. Bush and Gore both sent legal teams to Florida to oversee the process.

Some Florida counties had confusing ballots. In some cases, it wasn't clear whom people were voting for. In areas that voted heavily Democratic, there were a surprising number of ballots marked for a third-party candidate. Some people argued that the ballot design was confusing and that the votes really belonged to Gore. At the same time, some places had punch card ballots that weren't punched correctly, making it difficult to determine whom the person was voting for. This created many heated disagreements.

In December 2000, court cases made their way to the Florida Supreme Court, which ruled that questionable ballots in some Florida counties needed to be recounted by hand. The Bush team filed a suit with the US Supreme Court, which overturned the lower court's ruling and ended the recount. Then, in a 5–4 decision, the Supreme Court said a proper recount couldn't be conducted in time to meet a federal election deadline. This ruling gave Bush the presidency.

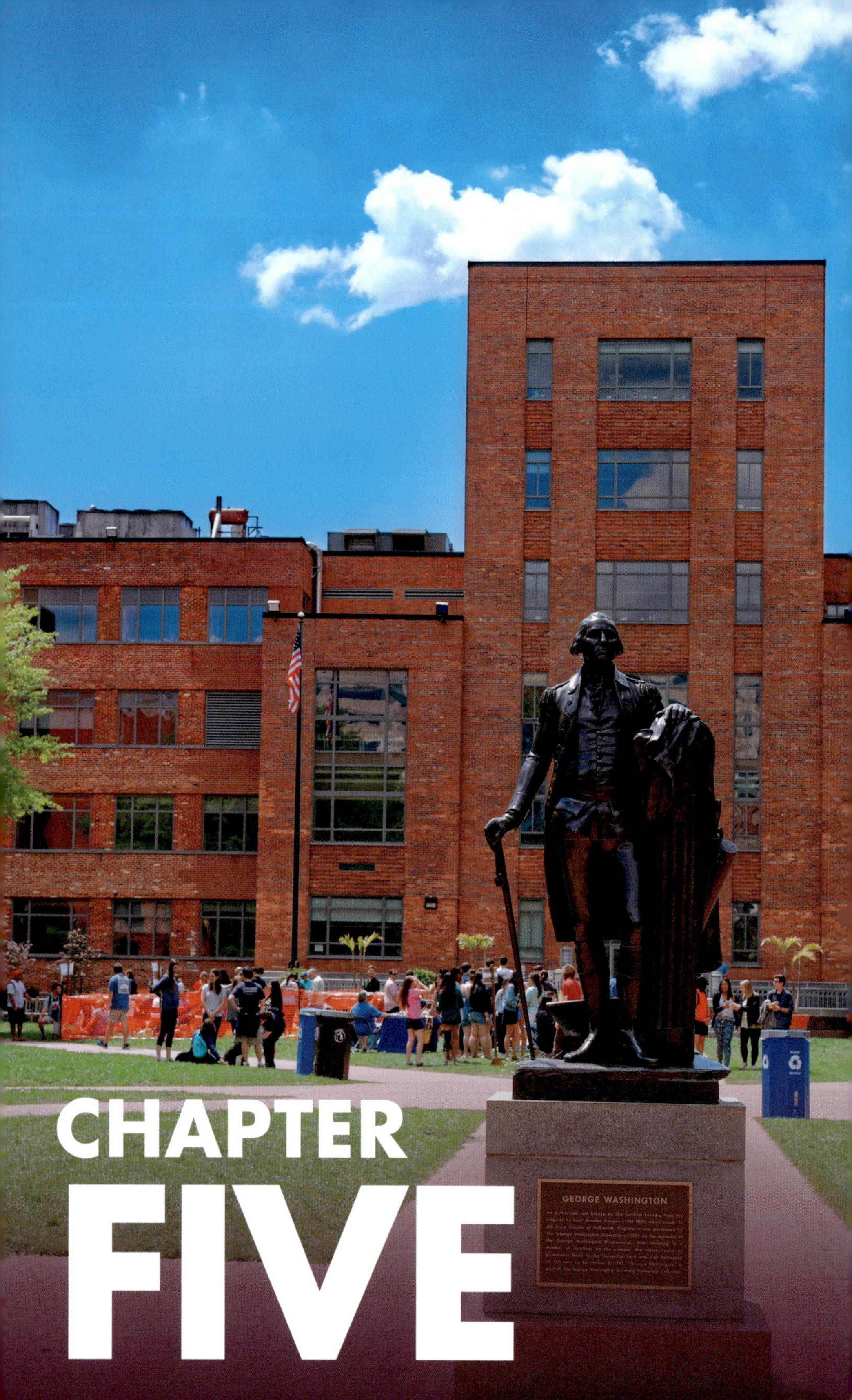

CHAPTER
FIVE
GEORGE WASHINGTON

PROFESSOR AND MOTHER

Although Barrett had enjoyed her time in private practice, she still had a strong desire to teach. In 2001, Barrett left Miller, Cassidy, Larroca & Lewin to take a teaching job at George Washington University Law School in Washington, DC. During her first year of teaching, Jesse and Barrett had their first child, a daughter named Emma. After Emma's birth, Barrett was unsure what her future career would look like. "I'd had my first baby and I felt terribly guilty leaving her in childcare to go in to work, and I thought 'should I stay home with her?'" said Barrett. "I felt a lot of anxiety about whether I was doing the best thing being away from Emma."[1]

As Barrett and Jesse worked to figure out how to balance both of their careers with homelife, Barrett's former professor William Kelley reached out to her. He was still teaching at Notre Dame and was part of a

Around 100,000 people live in South Bend.

movement to hire more conservative faculty members at the law school. Kelley asked Barrett to return to Notre Dame as a professor. Moving to South Bend would have many advantages. Jesse's family lived there, so they would be able to provide support and childcare when needed. Both Jesse and Barrett had friends there from their time as students. The job itself would provide flexibility, allowing Barrett to bring Emma to work if needed. She accepted the position. In 2002, Barrett, Jesse, and Emma moved to South Bend to start a new chapter in their lives.

A Homecoming

In many ways, returning to South Bend was a homecoming for the small family. Barrett and Jesse had both graduated from Notre Dame, and South Bend was also Jesse's hometown. However, that didn't mean the road ahead would be easy. Barrett recalled from her days as a student that the law school's professors were nearly all men. When visiting female professors did come to campus, she remembered her classmates being especially tough on them. Barrett wondered how she would be treated.

Another challenge Barrett faced was her age. Barrett was only 30 when she started teaching at Notre Dame. Many of her students were close in age to her. She worried they wouldn't take her seriously because she was so young compared to the other professors. "I wore my glasses when I taught to try to look very imposing," Barrett joked when recalling her early years as a professor.[2]

At this time, Barrett and her husband also had to figure out how to balance parenting and work. Barrett has spoken many times about how she and Jesse had to work as a team to make this happen. They both had

Jesse, *right*, became an assistant US attorney in the Northern District of Indiana in 2005.

demanding jobs and took turns running the household. Barrett also got creative with how she juggled her time. For instance, when Emma was young, Barrett recalled keeping a basket of toys in her office. That way she could have her daughter with her while she had student meetings.

Professor Barrett

As time passed, Barrett felt more confident in her role. She loved to teach and work with students, and she found the job rewarding. During her years at Notre Dame, she taught a variety of courses. Her favorites were those on public law. They focused on topics such as the federal courts and constitutional law. She also enjoyed teaching courses on civil procedure to first-year students. Civil procedures are the laws, methods, and standards that courts follow during trials. Some law students find this material dry. However, Barrett believed in its importance and worked hard to make it compelling for students. "Some of my teaching evaluations at the end of civil procedure would say things like, 'Wow, I'm so impressed you could make such a boring subject so interesting,' which I counted as a triumph," said Barrett.[3]

Barrett gained a reputation for her teaching methods,

such as holding mock trials. The students would be the lawyers, and Barrett would serve as the judge. During the mock trials, she kept her own opinions out of the classroom. Instead, Barrett focused on the content alone and pushed students to form their own opinions. Her former students recall her as being fair and open-minded, always trying to get them to explain their logic and expand upon their views. She often asked questions such as, "Why should I rule in your favor?"[5]

Methods like this quickly gained the attention and admiration of her students. "She would do things like that where she would bring in media clips or other things to kind of really drive the point home," said Libby Klesmith, one of Barrett's former students. "Her class was fun and engaging. She was one of those professors who really somehow found a way to make the subject matter stick in your brain." Another former student,

David Roberts, agreed, saying, "It's nice to actually go into class and have somebody who's really excited about the subject matter."[7]

Involvement with Conservative Groups

During her years as a professor, Barrett never actively became involved in politics, but she did have connections to many groups that were politically active. Some of these groups were faith based. For example, in 2006, Barrett and her husband joined hundreds of others in signing their names to an ad calling for the end of legal abortions. It appeared in the *South Bend Tribune*. The ad was sponsored by a pro-life group called St. Joseph County Right to Life. It stated, "We . . . oppose abortion on demand and defend the right to life from fertilization to natural death. Please continue to pray to end abortion."[8] Signing her name to this public ad showed Barrett's views on the hot button topic.

In 2015, Barrett once again signed her name to support the pro-life movement. It was a letter from female Catholic leaders to bishops of the Church. More than 1,300 women signed the letter, which affirmed "the dignity of the human person and the value of human

During the Supreme Court confirmation hearing, senators questioned Barrett's stance on abortion.

life from conception to natural death." This was a stance against the pro-choice position. The letter also affirmed the "meaning of human sexuality, the significance of sexual difference and the complementarity of men and women."[9] Many people interpreted this as a stance against the lesbian, gay, bisexual, transgender, and queer or questioning (LGBTQ) community and its rights.

Barrett's associations during this time were not all faith based. She also became a member of the Federalist Society. Conservative law students started the Federalist Society in the 1980s. Their goal was to form an organization that would help bring conservative legal ideas to their law schools. Since those days, the group has grown tremendously. It influences a number of legal issues across the nation, most notably in recommending conservative judges for federal appointments. All of the conservative justices who served on the Supreme Court in early 2021 had ties to the Federalist Society.

Barrett belonged to the Federalist Society from 2005 to 2006 and then again from 2014 to 2017. "It gave me the opportunity to speak to groups of interested, engaged students on topics of mutual interest," Barrett said of her membership in the group. "The Federalist Society's approach to public lectures is consistent with my approach to teaching. I don't tell my students what to think; I help them see the strengths and weaknesses of competing positions and let them choose. That is how Federalist Society talks work."[10]

Mom to Seven

While Barrett's involvement in teaching and faith-related issues was growing, so was her family. She and Jesse had five biological children. They also adopted two children from Haiti. Vivian was adopted in 2005, and John Peter was adopted five years later. Barrett describes their home as "a full house."[11] Over the years, many people have asked Barrett how she and Jesse have been able to manage a large family and demanding jobs. Barrett noted that she and Jesse go back and forth with their family responsibilities. When she is busy, he takes on more of the daily duties such as cooking and driving children to and from activities. In turn, she takes on more of these duties when Jesse's job is busy. It's a system they've worked on for years. She also gives a lot of credit to Jesse's aunt, who has provided childcare for the Barrett children since Emma was a baby.

It has not always been easy though. There were times when the task seemed overwhelming.

Barrett and six of her seven children visited the White House when she was nominated to the Supreme Court.

However, Barrett says she would not change anything about being such a busy mom. She says, "What greater thing can you do than raise children? That's where you have your greatest impact on the world."[12]

Barrett would also make an impact on the world beyond her roles as mother and professor. When President Trump took office in 2017, he was looking for conservative federal judges. Trump, along with legal advisers, created a list of potential candidates. Barrett's name was on that list, and from that point on her future would forever be altered.

CHAPTER
SIX

GAINING NATIONAL ATTENTION

After leaving Mass one day in February 2016, Barrett turned on her cell phone. A flood of messages awaited her. They all said the same thing: Justice Antonin Scalia had died. Scalia, whom she had clerked for shortly after completing law school, had been a mentor. His death was a shock. It also raised a number of questions about the future of the Supreme Court.

Replacing Scalia with a new justice would not be a smooth process. Hours after Scalia's death, Senate majority leader Mitch McConnell of Kentucky made a statement about Scalia's replacement. In it he said, "The American people should have a voice in the selection of their next Supreme Court justice. Therefore, this vacancy should not be filled until we have a new president."[1]

Barrett and other mourners said goodbye to Scalia as his casket rested in the Supreme Court's Great Hall.

President Barack Obama, *left*, and Senator Mitch McConnell, *right*, frequently disagreed on important issues while Obama was in office.

McConnell was referring to the presidential election that would take place about nine months later in November. At the time of Scalia's death, President Barack Obama was nearing the end of his second term. The country was preparing for an election, and the candidates, Hillary Clinton and Donald Trump, were deeply divided on many issues, along with the rest of the country. It was into this heated atmosphere that Obama put forth a nominee named Merrick Garland.

Typically, the nominee would go through a confirmation hearing in the Senate Judiciary Committee. Then its members would vote on whether to move the nomination to the Senate for final approval. But neither the hearing nor the Senate vote ever took place for Garland. Republicans controlled the Senate, and they didn't want Obama—a Democrat—to fill the Supreme Court vacancy. Republicans refused to move forward on Garland's nomination. Unlike Scalia, who was well known for his conservative legal views, Garland was a moderate. Many Republicans hoped Trump would win the election. Then as president, Trump would appoint a conservative justice to replace Scalia.

MERRICK GARLAND

Merrick Garland is a man whose name will be forever linked with the political discord between Democrats and Republicans in 2016. Garland grew up in Chicago, Illinois, and attended Harvard Law School. He clerked for Supreme Court justice William Brennan. Garland worked in private practice and later as a federal prosecutor. In 1997 he was confirmed to the Court of Appeals for the District of Columbia Circuit. After his blocked appointment to the Supreme Court, Garland returned to his job as a federal court judge. In 2021, Garland became the US attorney general under President Joe Biden.

This refusal stalled Garland's nomination process. McConnell agreed that it was the president's right to make a nomination, but he also argued that it was the Senate's right to withhold a confirmation. McConnell felt that the vacancy should remain open until the people had a chance to vote for who would become the next president. As a result, Garland's nomination never moved forward.

Barrett Explains the Garland Situation

On November 3, 2016, just days before Americans went to the polls to vote, Barrett gave a speech about the election's impact on the Supreme Court. She delivered her remarks to the Public Policy Institute at Jacksonville University in Florida. In the speech, she explained what was happening and why the replacement for Scalia's seat had created such a heated debate. Scalia's seat, she said, was significant because it could switch the balance of power on the court from liberal to conservative.

The true issue, Barrett maintained, was not just Scalia's seat. It was much bigger than that. Whoever won the next election as president could potentially make four appointments to the Supreme Court.

The first appointment would
be for Scalia's seat, which still
remained empty. But three
other justices looked to be
close to retirement. At the time
Barrett gave the speech, Justice
Ruth Bader Ginsburg was 83,
Justice Stephen Breyer was 78,
and Justice Anthony Kennedy
was 80. While justices can serve
for life, it seemed unlikely all
three of them would continue
on the court for much longer.
Since the court has only nine
justices, a president who makes
four appointments has the
power to nominate nearly half
of the court.

With Scalia's seat still empty, Americans went to the
polls to vote for president on November 8, 2016. Their
choice for president would be the person who would
nominate Scalia's replacement. Trump received more
electoral votes that Clinton, making him the winner.
Trump became the forty-fifth president of the United

States and took office on January 20, 2017. One of his first duties was to nominate a replacement for Scalia. On January 31, Trump nominated Neil Gorsuch for the position, and the Senate later confirmed him on April 7, 2017.

Judge Recommendations

The fight over Scalia's replacement had dominated the news in the months leading up to the election. Many Americans were aware of the tug-of-war going on between the two political parties. It was less well known how many other judicial appointments needed to be filled. When Trump took office, he had the task of appointing more than 100 judges on the lower federal courts.[2]

To advise him, Trump turned to White House Counsel

Neil Gorsuch, *front,* worked in the US Court of Appeals for the Tenth Circuit before joining the Supreme Court.

Donald F. McGahn II, whose job was to counsel Trump and his staff on legal matters related to the presidency. McGahn and Trump worked together closely. He gave the president recommendations on whom to nominate for each position. With McGahn's guidance, Trump tried to quickly fill openings with conservative judges.

Trump's ability to appoint so many judges happened because of a few specific circumstances. The first was due to the number of judges who had retired during the Obama administration and still needed to be replaced,

as well as judges who retired when Trump was in
office. The second had to do with politics. Republicans
controlled the presidency and the Senate. Members of
the Senate are responsible for confirming new judges.
Since the president and the majority of the senators
worked together as Republicans, the confirmations went
through quickly.

It was during this time that Barrett's name
repeatedly came up as a possible nominee for a position
as a federal appeals court judge. McGahn, who had gone
to law school at Notre Dame like Barrett, had heard
promising things about her. He heard these things not
only from Notre Dame connections but also through the
Federalist Society.

As McGahn learned more about Barrett, he believed
she'd be a good fit for a federal job. Her career was
top-notch. In addition to working as a clerk for Judge
Silberman and Justice Scalia, she had published a
number of journal articles and papers. They solidified
her conservative, originalist interpretation of the
Constitution. Her reputation as a professor was stellar.
In addition, Barrett had amassed a growing following in
the Federalist Society. Since this group helped identify
potential conservative judges, this connection became an

Donald McGahn, *left,* is a member of the Federalist Society.

asset to Barrett. Just weeks after taking office, Trump interviewed Barrett. It went well, and in the spring of 2017 Trump nominated her as a federal judge.

CHAPTER
SEVEN

FEDERAL JUDGE

President Trump nominated a slate of ten conservative judges for the lower federal courts in May 2017. According to McGahn, it was a fulfillment of Trump's promise "to appoint strong and principled jurists to the federal bench who will enforce the Constitution's limits on federal power and protect the liberty of all Americans."[1] Barrett was one of the nominees in this group. Trump nominated her to be a judge on the US Court of Appeals for the Seventh Circuit, which hears cases in Illinois, Indiana, and Wisconsin.

While Supreme Court nominees get more headlines, judges in the appeals courts are also very important. Few cases make it to the Supreme Court, and therefore a court of appeals makes the final ruling for most cases. As a result, the judges there play an important role in interpreting the law. Like a Supreme Court justice, a judge on a federal appeals court serves for a lifetime.

Barrett was a federal judge for three years before her Supreme Court nomination. She ruled on cases concerning privacy rights, gun rights, and more.

By July 2020, President Trump had appointed
almost 200 judges to federal courts.

Once a judge is appointed, his or her impact on the law
can last for many years.

Some Americans applauded Trump's slate of
conservative nominees, but not everyone was happy.
Critics suggested that Trump was taking advantage
of having control of the Senate to fill the courts with
conservative judges. The president of Alliance for
Justice, Nan Aron, condemned Trump's picks. "The
Trump administration has made clear its intention . . .
to pack the federal courts with ultraconservatives given a
stamp of approval by the Federalist Society," said Aron.[2]

The turmoil between Trump's followers and critics intensified as Barrett and her fellow nominees prepared for their confirmation hearings.

Confirmation Hearing

On September 6, 2017, Barrett testified before the Senate Judiciary Committee. Members of this committee asked her questions about her background, experiences, and views on judicial matters. It was not an easy interview. She faced tough questions not only about her legal viewpoints but also about her personal beliefs. Barrett had been outspoken regarding her Catholic

FILLING THE BENCH

In 2016, Trump campaigned on the idea of putting more conservative judges onto federal courts. Some people refer to this as filling the bench. It won over many conservative voters, because it meant Trump's influence would still be felt long after he left office. To fill the bench, Trump relied on advisers such as McGahn to identify conservative candidates. He also relied on elected lawmakers, especially McConnell. Trump's network created a streamlined process to nominate federal judges.

This effort reshaped the federal courts. According to McConnell, Trump's court appointments could be the president's most lasting legacy. "The impact that this administration could have on the courts is the most long-lasting impact we could have," said McConnell. This impact is exactly what concerned many Democrats. "They will way outlast most of us," said Democratic senator Richard Blumenthal of Connecticut, speaking of the judges filling the bench serving longer than lawmakers.[3]

faith in the past. Members of the committee focused on this. They wondered whether her personal beliefs would get in the way of making legal judgments.

One of the first questions regarding this issue came from Senator Chuck Grassley of Iowa. He asked Barrett about a piece of writing she had done just before graduating from law school. She had partnered with one of her professors, John Garvey, to write an article called "Catholic Judges in Capital Cases." It appeared in the *Marquette Law Review* in 1998. The article had put forth the idea that in cases requiring the death penalty, Catholic judges may need to recuse themselves. When judges recuse themselves, it means they remove themselves from the case. They do this if they have a conflict of interest and would not be able to make unbiased judgments. In this situation, Catholic teachings are in conflict with the death penalty.

This idea of what is more important to a judge—personal beliefs or laws—became the main line of questioning for Barrett. Throughout the hearing, Democratic members of the committee asked Barrett in a variety of ways how her faith would affect her work as a judge. She repeatedly stated that her faith would not stand in the way of making legal judgments. If that were not possible in a case, she would recuse herself. When pressed further Barrett stated, "If you're asking whether I take my faith seriously and I'm a faithful Catholic, I am. Although, I would stress that my personal church affiliation or my religious belief would not bear in the discharge of my duties as a judge."[5]

California senator Dianne Feinstein raised concerns about Barrett's ability to break from the Catholic Church's teachings. "When you read your speeches, the conclusion one draws is that the dogma lives loudly within you," said Feinstein. "And that's of concern."[6] Feinstein was referring to the dogma associated with Barrett's faith. In this case, dogma is a set of beliefs that an authority—such as the Catholic Church—sets out as absolutely true. In saying this, Feinstein indicated

Some political and religious leaders took issue with Senator Dianne Feinstein asking questions regarding Barrett's faith.

concern that Barrett would not be able to lay aside her personal beliefs if they did not agree with the law. Despite the heat from Feinstein and other Democrats, the Senate confirmed Barrett as a federal judge on October 31, 2017, with a vote of 55–43.

Working As a Judge

That fall, Barrett began work as a judge on the US Court of Appeals for the Seventh Circuit. The United States has 13 courts of appeals. Each one is made up of

between six and 29 judges, depending on the circuit. A
panel of three judges is randomly selected to hear each
case. Their jobs are to hear
cases that have already gone
to trial. If one of the parties
disagrees with the outcome
of a case at the district court
level, the party can appeal
to the circuit court level.
The judges on the court of
appeals decide whether the
law in that first trial had been
properly applied.

Barrett worked as a
court of appeals judge for
three years. This is a relatively short amount of time to
establish a judicial record, but Barrett did hear a number
of cases involving contentious topics. Most of her record
showed her application of the originalist interpretation
of the law. The way she judged these cases, and the
opinions she wrote, provided some clues as to how she
might judge future cases.

For example, in 2019 Barrett wrote a dissenting
opinion in the case of *Kanter v. Barr.* The case was

JUDGE DOGMA

Dianne Feinstein's comment
that "the dogma lives
loudly within you" turned
Barrett into a hero in
conservative circles. She
has come to represent
pride in the Catholic faith.
Feinstein's dogma comment
has been splashed across
mugs, T-shirts, and other
merchandise. "We now
affectionately call her Judge
Dogma," McGahn said
of Barrett.[7]

about gun rights. Rickey Kanter of Wisconsin had been convicted of mail fraud, which is a felony. Under federal law and Wisconsin state law, felons cannot own firearms. Kanter appealed this ruling, saying that his Second Amendment right to own firearms was being violated. Two of the appeals court judges ruled against Kanter. But Barrett wrote a 37-page dissent on the case using an originalist perspective. She argued that since Kanter's crime had not been violent, it shouldn't automatically disqualify him from owning a firearm.

Barrett's conservative opinions on other cases involving abortion, sexual assault, and immigration gained a growing amount of attention from Republican leaders in Washington, DC. Just two weeks after her confirmation as a judge, McGahn began to place Barrett's name on Trump's running list of potential justices for the Supreme Court. When Justice Anthony Kennedy retired in 2018, Barrett's name

Brett Kavanaugh, *left*, had his swearing-in
ceremony in early October 2018.

circulated as a possible replacement. The position

ultimately went to Brett Kavanaugh. But McGahn and

Trump had big plans for Barrett.

CHAPTER
EIGHT

SUPREME COURT JUSTICE

Late in the afternoon of September 26, 2020, the weather in Washington, DC, looked threatening. Dark clouds gathered overhead, and the air felt sticky with humidity. For some people gathered at the White House's Rose Garden, the weather felt symbolic of the difficult events of the past few weeks. Memorial services for Justice Ruth Bader Ginsburg, who died earlier that month, had just taken place. A presidential debate scheduled for the next week loomed ahead. The world was also in the midst of a pandemic. A disease called COVID-19 was running rampant around the world and had killed hundreds of thousands of Americans.

President Trump wanted to get his nomination for the next Supreme Court justice through the Senate before his term ended in just a few months. People had gathered at the Rose Garden to hear him formally announce his selection. Despite the threatening skies,

Barrett promised to uphold the US Constitution as a Supreme Court justice.

guests took their places and Trump, joined by Barrett and her family, walked out to welcome the crowd. Trump and Barrett were greeted by a long roar of applause. After her calm, cool responses during a rocky confirmation hearing in 2017, Barrett had become somewhat of a hero to many conservatives. They hoped she would follow in Scalia's footsteps, and they were excited to see her as Trump's third nomination to the highest court.

Trump spoke to the assembled crowd, highlighting Barrett's background in the law and why he chose to nominate her. He then turned the microphone over to Barrett so she could share her own thoughts on the nomination and what it meant to her. "The President has nominated me to serve on the United States Supreme Court, and that institution belongs to all of us," Barrett said. "If confirmed, I would not assume that role for the sake of those in my own circle, and certainly not for my own sake. I would assume this role to serve you. I would discharge the judicial oath, which requires me to administer justice without respect to persons, do equal right to the poor and rich, and faithfully and impartially discharge my duties under the United States Constitution."[1]

Many people attended Barrett's nomination event.

After Barrett finished speaking, Trump made one last remark, this time to the senators who had gathered at the Rose Garden. "I know you're going to have a busy couple of weeks, but I think it's going to be easier than you might think," he said regarding getting Barrett's nomination approved by the Senate.[2] With that, Trump and the Barrett family left the Rose Garden and entered the White House. The next phase of Barrett's career was underway. Despite Trump's optimistic remarks, no one knew exactly what the process ahead would entail.

Disagreements Heat Up

Almost immediately after Barrett's nomination, disagreements between Republicans and Democrats heated up. Democrats brought up former president Barack Obama's 2016 nomination of Merrick Garland during an election year. Obama had 11 months left in office when he nominated Garland. Republicans, led by Senator Mitch McConnell, had blocked Garland's hearing, saying it was too close to an election to confirm a new justice. Now in 2020, many of the same Republicans who succeeded in blocking Garland wanted to move Trump's nominee through the process during an election year. In Barrett's case, her nomination

SUPER-SPREADER EVENT

When guests gathered at the Rose Garden for Barrett's nomination, the nation was in the middle of the COVID-19 pandemic. The decision to wear masks to stop the spread of COVID-19 had become political. Some people, including President Trump, had been slow to adopt the practice. Many of the people at the Rose Garden event also chose not to wear masks. In addition, the chairs people sat in were not placed six feet (1.8 m) apart—the spacing recommended by health experts to stop the spread of COVID-19. Days later, an outbreak of the disease occurred among the guests at the event. Nearly 40 of the people who had attended tested positive for the virus, including President Trump.[3] Barrett's nomination had become a super-spreader event during the pandemic.

came when Trump had less than four months left in his first term.

Led by McConnell, Republicans worked to push Barrett's confirmation through the Senate quickly. McConnell defended this decision early in the process. He said that the situations in the Garland and Barrett nominations were different. When Garland was nominated, the presidency and Senate were controlled by different parties. McConnell said that historically, justices were not confirmed during an election year when the government was divided. During Barrett's nomination, Republicans controlled both the presidency and the Senate.

Democrats cried foul. Joe Biden, Obama's former vice president and the 2020 presidential candidate for the Democratic Party, issued a statement regarding this issue. "The American people know the US Supreme Court decisions affect their everyday lives," wrote Biden. "The United States Constitution was designed to give the voters one chance to have their voice heard on who serves on the Court. That moment is now and their voice should be heard. The Senate should not act on this vacancy until after the American people select their next president and the next Congress."[4]

Joe Biden won more electoral votes than Donald Trump in the 2020 presidential election. Biden became the forty-sixth US president on January 20, 2021.

Despite the efforts of Biden and other Democrats, Barrett's confirmation moved forward. The confirmation hearing was scheduled for October 12, 2020. This made Barrett the first justice in history to undergo a confirmation after July 1 of an election year.

This decision was met with an outcry from Democrats. "[McConnell has] destroyed the orderly process of selecting judicial nominees," said Illinois senator Dick Durbin.[5] McConnell defended his decision. He said Republicans had simply used "the power that was given to us by the American people, in a manner that is entirely within the rules of the Senate and the Constitution of the United States."[6]

The ACA and Super Precedents

It was into this intensely divided atmosphere that Barrett prepared to testify before the Senate Judiciary Committee. At nine o'clock a.m. on October 12, Senator Lindsey Graham of South Carolina called the hearing to order. Over the next three days, Barrett answered questions from the committee's 22 members.

Many members tried to pin Barrett down on certain issues, but she calmy resisted sharing her personal opinions. This is not unusual for a nominee. Like nominees before her, Barrett maintained that it would be unethical to share an opinion on an issue that might appear before her on the bench.

Unlike in her hearing to become a circuit court judge, this hearing did not focus so tightly on her faith. Instead, members spent much more of their time asking her about the Affordable Care Act (ACA). The ACA was the subject of a case the Supreme Court planned to hear on November 10—just a week after the election. The ACA is a health-care reform law that was passed in 2010. It's sometimes called Obamacare, since it was passed during Obama's presidency. The ACA strives to make health insurance more affordable while also expanding health-care programs, such as Medicaid.

Some members of the Senate Judiciary Committee wanted to know how Barrett might vote on it. The law was less than ten years old when she began working on the circuit court. During her time there, she did not rule on any cases involving the ACA. But when a case against the ACA appeared before the Supreme Court in 2017, she wrote a legal criticism of it. The article

During Barrett's hearing, some Democratic senators voiced concerns about what they felt was at stake if the Supreme Court had a strong conservative leaning.

appeared in a journal published by Notre Dame Law School. Members of the committee wondered whether her criticism meant she would strike down the ACA if she became a justice. Many Republicans were in favor of ending the ACA. Democrats, on the other hand, wanted to make sure it remained a law. Committee members grilled Barrett on her opinion, but Barrett maintained repeatedly that she was "not on a mission to destroy the Affordable Care Act."[8] Despite this, Senator Durbin reminded all who were listening that Trump's position on the ACA was clear—he wanted it repealed. Since Trump nominated Barrett, Durbin declared, Trump's agenda to repeal the ACA hung over Barrett's confirmation process.

Another topic of questioning for Barrett was about super precedents. These are cases that are so widely accepted that no one is actively appealing them anymore. As a result, they are regarded as established laws and are very unlikely to be overturned. When Minnesota senator Amy Klobuchar asked Barrett about super precedents, she brought up *Roe v. Wade*. "*Roe* is not a super precedent because calls for its overruling have never ceased, but that doesn't mean *Roe* should be overruled,"

said Barrett.[9] That answer led many to believe Barrett was open to hearing challenges to the case. A lot of people were concerned that *Roe v. Wade* could potentially be overturned.

Barrett also answered questions about what would happen if a case regarding the 2020 presidential election arrived at the Supreme Court. If this happened, the case could have the potential to determine the outcome of

Supreme Court justices take two oaths of office. One is the constitutional oath, which Barrett took on October 26. The other is the judicial oath, which she took the next day.

the election as it did in 2000. Many wondered whether Barrett's loyalties would lie with Trump, who not only nominated her but pushed to get her confirmed quickly before the election. Barrett said she would follow the process judges undergo when deciding whether they need to recuse themselves from a case, but she also pushed back on the question. "I certainly hope that all members of the committee have more confidence in my integrity than to think I would allow myself to be used as a pawn to decide this election for the American people," Barrett said.[10]

Confirmation Vote

After Barrett's hearing, the next step was for the committee to vote. Then its members could send Barrett's nomination to the full Senate. Democrats on the committee boycotted the vote in protest. Despite this, the committee's final vote had 12 for Barrett, which was enough to advance the nomination to the Senate.

The vote in the full Senate took place on October 26, 2020. As many people expected, the votes fell largely along party lines, and Barrett won confirmation to the Supreme Court. With that, the Supreme Court's balance of power shifted. It now had a 6–3 majority of conservative judges. With Barrett being only 48 years old at the time of her swearing in, she had the potential to affect the court for decades.

Even before her appointment to the Supreme Court, Barrett had a distinguished career. During her time as a professor at Notre Dame, she taught difficult content while also engaging students and challenging them to do their best. As a federal judge, she used her knowledge of the law to pass down judgments on a wide variety of cases. However, she faced criticism from opponents regarding her nominations to both the court of appeals and the Supreme Court. Most of these critiques centered on her faith, her ties to conservative groups, and her originalist interpretation of the Constitution. Her nomination and confirmation happened amid a firestorm of national politics. Many conservatives praised her appointment, hoping she would decide cases in ways that matched their views. People throughout the United States took notice of Barrett and wondered how the new justice would make her mark in the country's highest court.

TIMELINE

1972

Amy Vivian Coney is born on January 28 in Metairie, Louisiana.

1990

Barrett graduates from St. Mary's Dominican High School.

1994

Barrett graduates from Rhodes College with an English degree; she contemplates continuing school to become an English professor but ultimately decides to go to law school.

1997

Barrett graduates at the top her class from Notre Dame Law School; she works as a clerk for Judge Laurence H. Silberman on the US Court of Appeals for the District of Columbia Circuit.

1998

Barrett works as a law clerk for Supreme
Court justice Antonin Scalia.

1999

Barrett gets married; she takes a job at a
private law firm near Washington, DC.

2000

Barrett works on the high-profile case *Bush v.
Gore*, a case related to the presidential election
and that the Supreme Court ultimately ruled on.

2001

Barrett takes a teaching position at George
Washington University Law School; Emma is born.

2002

Barrett leaves her position at George Washington
University Law School and becomes a professor
at her alma mater, Notre Dame Law School.

TIMELINE

2005

Barrett joins the Federalist Society for the first time; the Barrett family adopts Vivian.

2006

Barrett and her husband sign their names to a pro-life ad.

2015

Barrett signs her name to a pro-life letter to bishops of the Catholic Church.

2016

Justice Antonin Scalia, Barrett's mentor, dies; Barrett gives a speech about how the 2016 election could impact the Supreme Court.

2017

President Donald Trump nominates Barrett to be a federal judge; on October 31, the Senate approves Barrett as a judge on the US Court of Appeals for the Seventh Circuit.

2018

Following Justice Anthony Kennedy's retirement,
Barrett's name appears on Trump's short list
of nominees for the Supreme Court, but he
ultimately chooses Brett Kavanaugh instead.

2019

Barrett attends an event called "A Conversation with
Judge Amy Coney Barrett" to discuss her personal
life and work as a federal judge; she is the sole
dissenting judge on the case *Kanter v. Barr*.

2020

Justice Ruth Bader Ginsburg dies on September 18,
leaving an opening on the Supreme Court; on
September 26, Trump nominates Barrett as the next
Supreme Court justice; Barrett's confirmation hearing
begins on October 12; the Senate votes to confirm
Barrett to the Supreme Court on October 26.

ESSENTIAL FACTS

Date of Birth
January 28, 1972

Place of Birth
Metairie, Louisiana

Parents
Michael and Linda Coney

Education
Rhodes College
Notre Dame Law School

Marriage
Jesse Barrett (1999)

Children
Emma, Vivian, Tess, John Peter, Liam, Juliet, and Benjamin

Career Highlights
Barrett worked as a law clerk for Judge Laurence H. Silberman. She later earned a prestigious position as a clerk for Supreme Court justice Antonin Scalia. Barrett became a professor at George Washington University Law School and later at Notre Dame Law School. In 2017, Barrett started working as a federal judge on the US Court of Appeals for the Seventh Circuit. In 2020, she was sworn in as a justice on the US Supreme Court.

Societal Contributions

As a professor, Barrett worked hard to engage students. As
a federal judge, she oversaw many cases and used her
originalist view of the Constitution to apply the rule of law.
Barrett's position on the Supreme Court makes her the fifth
woman to rise to that role. In addition to her work in the
classroom and in the courts, Barrett has added her name to
various pro-life movements that align with her Catholic faith.

Conflicts

Barrett and her husband had to work together in order
to balance their large family with their demanding jobs.
In 2017, Barrett encountered questions regarding her
Catholic faith as an impediment to her ability to judge cases
objectively. In 2020, Barrett was swept into a political
firestorm between Republicans and Democrats as the parties
argued over whether a Supreme Court vacancy should be
filled just a few months before a presidential election.

Quote

"I never imagined that I would find myself in this position.
But now that I am, I assure you that I will meet the challenge
with both humility and courage."—*Amy Coney Barrett,
September 26, 2020, during her nomination for the Supreme Court*

GLOSSARY

appeal
A request for a higher court to review the decision of a lower court.

aptitude
A natural ability to do something or learn something.

attorney general
The head law officer in either a country or state.

blue book
A small, blank notebook used for essay exams in high schools and colleges.

brief
A written summary of a legal case to be presented to a court.

deposition
A formal, written statement from a witness sometimes used in a court of law.

dissenting opinion
An opinion that differs from the majority opinion in a court ruling.

marginalized
Excluded or treated as unimportant or of a lower class.

Medicaid
A health insurance program established in 1965 to assist children, pregnant women, and families as well as people with disabilities or blindness.

moderate
A person who holds political beliefs that are not extreme.

parish
A specific district in a church community that usually has its own church and priest or pastor.

pro-choice
Believing in a woman's right to choose whether she should have a baby or have an abortion.

pro-life
Believing that a fetus is a human child and should not be aborted.

prosecute
To conduct legal proceedings against someone accused of a crime.

ratify
To formally approve or adopt an idea or document.

solicitor general
A law officer who helps an attorney general; sometimes the head law officer in a state.

ADDITIONAL RESOURCES

Selected Bibliography

"Amy Coney Barrett, in Her Own Words." *Heritage Foundation*, 28 Sept. 2020, heritage.org. Accessed 15 Dec. 2020.

Dias, Elizabeth, et al. "Rooted in Faith, Amy Coney Barrett Represents a New Conservatism." *New York Times*, 14 Oct. 2020, nytimes.com. Accessed 12 Jan. 2021.

Grimaldi, James V., et al. "Amy Coney Barrett's Intellectual Firepower, Conservative Mentors Propelled Career." *Wall Street Journal,* 11 Oct. 2020, wsj.com. Accessed 15 Dec. 2020.

Further Readings

Harris, Duchess. *Freedom of Religion*. Abdo, 2018.

Reston, Dominick. *Donald Trump: 45th US President*. ReferencePoint, 2017.

Streissguth, Tom. *The 2016 Presidential Election*. Abdo, 2018.

Online Resources

To learn more about Amy Coney Barrett, please visit **abdobooklinks.com** or scan this QR code. These links are routinely monitored and updated to provide the most current information available.

Administrative Office of the United States Courts

1 Columbus Cir. NE

Washington, DC 20544

uscourts.gov

This site has information on the federal government's judicial branch, including information on district and circuit courts, as well as educational resources.

National Constitution Center

525 Arch St.

Philadelphia, PA 19106

215-409-6600

constitutioncenter.org

This site provides an interactive version of the Constitution, a virtual museum, as well as other resources such as podcasts and blogs written by constitutional scholars.

Supreme Court of the United States

1 First St. NE

Washington, DC 20543

202-479-3030

supremecourt.gov

The official government site of the Supreme Court of the United States has information on the court's history, its rulings, and its past and present justices.

SOURCE NOTES

Chapter 1. A New Justice

1. "Remarks by President Trump at Swearing-In Ceremony of the Honorable Amy Coney Barrett as Associate Justice of the Supreme Court of the United States." *Trump White House*, 26 Oct. 2020, trumpwhitehouse.archives.gov. Accessed 28 Jan. 2021.

2. "Remarks by President Trump."

3. "Oath of Office." *United States Senate*, n.d., senate.gov. Accessed 28 Jan. 2021.

4. "Nomination: A Historical Overview." *United States Senate*, n.d., senate.gov. Accessed 22 Feb. 2021.

5. Tamara Keith. "'Titan of the Law': Trump Reacts to Ginsburg's Death." *NPR*, 18 Sept. 2020, npr.org. Accessed 28 Jan. 2021.

6. "Remarks by President Trump Announcing His Nominee for Associate Justice of the Supreme Court of the United States." *Trump White House*, 26 Sept. 2020, trumpwhitehouse.archives.gov. Accessed 28 Jan. 2021.

Chapter 2. Growing Up

1. Notre Dame Law School. "A Conversation with Judge Amy Coney Barrett '97 J.D. (Full Interview)." *YouTube*, 8 Aug. 2019, youtube.com. Accessed 28 Jan. 2021.

2. Jeff Parrott. "Supreme Court Opening Shines Spotlight on Local Religious Group People of Praise." *South Bend Tribune*, 15 July 2018, southbendtribune.com. Accessed 28 Jan. 2021.

3. Ruth Graham and Sharon LaFraniere. "Inside the People of Praise, the Tight-Knit Faith Community of Amy Coney Barrett." *New York Times*, 8 Oct. 2020, nytimes.com. Accessed 28 Jan. 2021.

4. "Who We Are." *People of Praise*, n.d., peopleofpraise.org. Accessed 28 Jan. 2021.

5. "FAQ: What Is the People of Praise?" *People of Praise*, n.d., peopleofpraise.org. Accessed 28 Jan. 2021.

6. Graham and LaFraniere, "Inside the People of Praise."

7. Graham and LaFraniere, "Inside the People of Praise."

8. Notre Dame Law School, "A Conversation with Judge Amy Coney Barrett."

9. "Rhodes College Alumna Amy Coney Barrett '94 Confirmed to the Supreme Court of the United States." *Rhodes College*, 26 Oct. 2020, news.rhodes.edu. Accessed 28 Jan. 2021.

10. Notre Dame Law School, "A Conversation with Judge Amy Coney Barrett."

Chapter 3. Notre Dame Law School

1. John Kass and Jeff Carlin. "Why Amy Coney Barrett's Former Law Professor Isn't Surprised She's Headed to the Supreme Court." *WGN Radio 720*, 13 Oct. 2020, wgnradio.com. Accessed 28 Jan. 2021.

2. John Garvey. "I Taught and Worked with Amy Coney Barrett. Here's What People Get Wrong about Her Faith." *Washington Post*, 25 Sept. 2020, washingtonpost.com. Accessed 28 Jan. 2021.

3. Notre Dame Law School. "A Conversation with Judge Amy Coney Barrett '97 J.D. (Full Interview)." *YouTube*, 8 Aug. 2019, youtube.com. Accessed 28 Jan. 2021.

4. Neil M. Gorsuch. "Justice Neil Gorsuch: Why Originalism Is the Best Approach to the Constitution." *Time*, 6 Sept. 2019, time.com. Accessed 28 Jan. 2021.

5. Glenn Smith. "What's a Constitutional 'Originalist'?" *San Diego State University*, n.d., ces.sdsu.edu. Accessed 28 Jan. 2021.

6. Katie Vloet. "Two Views of the Constitution: Originalism vs. Non-Originalism." *Michigan Law*, 22 Sept. 2015, law.umich.edu. Accessed 28 Jan. 2021.

7. "A Conversation with Amy Coney Barrett." *Hillsdale College*, 21 May 2019, hillsdale.edu. Accessed 28 Jan. 2021.

Chapter 4. Life as a Clerk

1. James V. Grimaldi et al. "Amy Coney Barrett's Intellectual Firepower, Conservative Mentors Propelled Career." *Wall Street Journal*, 11 Oct. 2020, wsj.com. Accessed 28 Jan. 2021.

2. Elizabeth Dias et al. "Rooted in Faith, Amy Coney Barrett Represents a New Conservatism." *New York Times*, 14 Oct. 2020, nytimes.com. Accessed 28 Jan. 2021.

3. Michael Kranish et al. "Amy Coney Barrett, a Disciple of Justice Scalia, Is Poised to Push the Supreme Court Further Right." *Washington Post*, 26 Sept. 2020, washingtonpost.com. Accessed 28 Jan. 2021.

4. Eva Barkoff. "What Amy Coney Barrett Told the *Times-Picayune* When She Started Clerking for Scalia in 1997." *Nola*, 28 Sept. 2020, nola.com. Accessed 28 Jan. 2021.

5. "About the Supreme Court." *US Courts*, n.d., uscourts.gov. Accessed 28 Jan. 2021.

6. "Amy Coney Barrett, in Her Own Words." *Heritage Foundation*, 28 Sept. 2020, heritage.org. Accessed 28 Jan. 2021.

7. "Amy Coney Barrett, in Her Own Words."

8. Richard Wolf. "Opera, Travel, Food, Law: The Unlikely Friendship of Ruth Bader Ginsburg and Antonin Scalia." *USA Today*, 20 Sept. 2020, usatoday.com. Accessed 28 Jan. 2021.

9. Jacksonville University. "Hesburgh Lecture 2016: Professor Amy Barrett at the JU Public Policy Institute." *YouTube*, 5 Dec. 2016, youtube.com. Accessed 28 Jan. 2021.

10. Andrew Maloney. "The Big Law Background of Trump's Pool of Supreme Court Candidates." *American Lawyer*, 22 Sept. 2020, law.com. Accessed 28 Jan. 2021.

11. Doyle McManus et al. "Bush Wins, Gore Wins—Depending on How Ballots Are Added Up." *Chicago Tribune*, 13 Nov. 2001, chicagotribune.com. Accessed 28 Jan. 2021.

Chapter 5. Professor and Mother

1. Notre Dame Law School. "A Conversation with Judge Amy Coney Barrett '97 J.D. (Full Interview)." *YouTube*, 8 Aug. 2019, youtube.com. Accessed 28 Jan. 2021.

2. Notre Dame Law School, "A Conversation with Judge Amy Coney Barrett."

3. "Amy Coney Barrett, in Her Own Words." *Heritage Foundation*, 28 Sept. 2020, heritage.org. Accessed 28 Jan. 2021.

4. Laura E. Wolk et al. "Amy Coney Barrett Was Our Professor. She'll Serve America As Well As She Served Her Students." *USA Today*, 27 Sept. 2020, usatoday.com. Accessed 28 Jan. 2021.

SOURCE NOTES CONTINUED

5. Patrick Smith. "Amy Coney Barrett's Notre Dame Students and Colleagues Weigh In on Possible Supreme Court Nominee." *WBEZ Chicago*, 24 Sept. 2020, wbez.org. Accessed 28 Jan. 2021.

6. Dennis Brown. "Notre Dame Law School Professor Barrett Nominated to US Supreme Court." *University of Notre Dame*, 26 Sept. 2020, news.nd.edu. Accessed 28 Jan. 2021.

7. Smith, "Amy Coney Barrett's Notre Dame Students and Colleagues Weigh In."

8. Stephanie Kirchgaessner. "Revealed: Amy Coney Barrett Supported Group That Said Life Begins at Fertilization." *Guardian*, 1 Oct. 2020, amp.theguardian.com. Accessed 28 Jan. 2021.

9. "Letter to Synod Fathers from Catholic Women." *Ethics & Public Policy Center*, 1 Oct. 2015, eppc.org. Accessed 28 Jan. 2021.

10. "Senator Dick Durbin's Written Questions for Amy Coney Barrett." *Committee on the Judiciary*, 13 Sept. 2017, judiciary.senate.gov. Accessed 28 Jan. 2021.

11. Notre Dame Law School, "A Conversation with Judge Amy Coney Barrett."

12. Notre Dame Law School, "A Conversation with Judge Amy Coney Barrett."

Chapter 6. Gaining National Attention

1. Jason Silverstein. "Here's What Mitch McConnell Said about Not Filing a Supreme Court Vacancy in an Election Year." *CBS News*, 19 Sept. 2020, cbsnews.com. Accessed 28 Jan. 2021.

2. Philip Rucker and Robert Barnes. "Trump to Inherit More Than 100 Court Vacancies, Plans to Reshape Judiciary." *Washington Post*, 25 Dec. 2016, washingtonpost.com. Accessed 28 Jan. 2021.

3. "Supreme Court Nominations, 1789 to 2018: Actions by the Senate, the Judiciary Committee, and the President." *Federation of American Scientists*, 9 Oct. 2020, fas.org. Accessed 28 Jan. 2021.

Chapter 7. Federal Judge

1. Adam Liptak. "Trump to Announce Slate of Conservative Federal Court Nominees." *New York Times,* 7 May 2017, nytimes.com. Accessed 28 Jan. 2021.

2. Liptak, "Trump to Announce Slate of Conservative Federal Court Nominees."

3. Tessa Berenson. "Inside Trump's Plan to Dramatically Reshape US Courts." *Time*, 8 Feb. 2018, time.com. Accessed 28 Jan. 2021.

4. "Article VI, Clause 3." *Constitution Annotated*, n.d., constitution.congress.gov. Accessed 28 Jan. 2021.

5. "Judicial and Justice Department Pending Nominations." *C-SPAN*, 6 Sept. 2017, c-span.org. Accessed 28 Jan. 2021.

6. "Feinstein: 'The Dogma Lives Loudly within You, and That's a Concern.'" *C-SPAN*, 7 Sept. 2017, c-span.org. Accessed 28 Jan. 2021.

7. Elizabeth Dias et al. "Rooted in Faith, Amy Coney Barrett Represents a New Conservatism." *New York Times*, 14 Oct. 2020, nytimes.com. Accessed 28 Jan. 2021.

8. "Court Role and Structure." *US Courts*, n.d., uscourts.gov. Accessed 28 Jan. 2021.

9. "About the Supreme Court." *US Courts*, n.d., uscourts.gov. Accessed 28 Jan. 2021.

Chapter 8. Supreme Court Justice

1. "Remarks by President Trump Announcing His Nominee for Associate Justice of the Supreme Court of the United States." *Trump White House*, 26 Sept. 2020, trumpwhitehouse.archives.gov. Accessed 28 Jan. 2021.

2. "Remarks by President Trump Announcing His Nominee."

3. Matthew Impelli. "Amy Coney Barrett Rose Garden Event Was a WH COVID Superspreader, New Data Suggests." *Newsweek*, 9 Oct. 2020, newsweek.com. Accessed 28 Jan. 2021.

4. "The US Supreme Court—Statement by Vice President Joe Biden." *Joe Biden*, 26 Sept. 2020, joebiden.com. Accessed 28 Jan. 2021.

5. John Bresnahan and Burgess Everett. "No Apologies: McConnell Says Barrett a 'Huge Success for the Country.'" *Politico*, 27 Oct. 2020, politico.com. Accessed 28 Jan. 2021.

6. Tucker Higgins. "Amy Coney Barrett Is Sworn In, Swinging Supreme Court Further to the Right." *CNBC*, 26 Oct. 2020, cnbc.com. Accessed 28 Jan. 2021.

7. "Supreme Court Appointment Process: Senate Debate and Confirmation Vote." *Federation of American Scientists*, 16 Oct. 2020, fas.org. Accessed 28 Jan. 2021.

8. Deirdre Walsh. "Takeaways from Amy Coney Barrett's Judiciary Confirmation Hearings." *NPR*, 15 Oct. 2020, npr.org. Accessed 28 Jan. 2021.

9. Walsh, "Takeaways from Amy Coney Barrett's Judiciary Confirmation Hearings."

10. Walsh, "Takeaways from Amy Coney Barrett's Judiciary Confirmation Hearings."

INDEX

ABOUT THE AUTHOR

Kate Conley

Kate Conley has been writing nonfiction books for children
for more than a decade. When she's not writing, Conley
spends her time reading, drawing, and solving crossword
puzzles. She lives in Minnesota with her husband and two
children.

ABOUT THE CONSULTANT

Scott S. Boddery, JD, PhD

Scott S. Boddery, JD, PhD, is an expert in judicial politics
and court legitimacy. His scholarship and commentary on
the US Supreme Court have appeared in a wide array of
popular presses and scholarly journals. He is an assistant
professor of political science and public law at Gettysburg
College in Pennsylvania. He lives in the area with his wife
and three dogs.